NEXT LIFE

other books by the author

POETRY
Dawn Visions
Burnt Heart/Ode to the War Dead
This Body of Black Light Gone Through the Diamond
The Desert is the Only Way Out
The Chronicles of Akhira
The Blind Beekeeper
Mars & Beyond
Laughing Buddha Weeping Sufi
Salt Prayers
Ramadan Sonnets
Psalms for the Brokenhearted
I Imagine a Lion
Coattails of the Saint
Abdallah Jones and the Disappearing-Dust Caper (illustrated by the author)
Love is a Letter Burning in a High Wind
The Flame of Transformation Turns to Light
Underwater Galaxies
The Music Space
Cooked Oranges
Through Rose Colored Glasses
Like When You Wave at a Train and the Train Hoots Back at You
In the Realm of Neither
The Fire Eater's Lunchbreak
Millennial Prognostications
You Open a Door and it's a Starry Night
Where Death Goes
Shaking the Quicksilver Pool
The Perfect Orchestra
Sparrow on the Prophet's Tomb
A Maddening Disregard for the Passage of Time
Stretched Out on Amethysts
Invention of the Wheel
Sparks Off the Main Strike
Chants for the Beauty Feast
In Constant Incandescence
Holiday from the Perfect Crime
The Caged Bear Spies the Angel
The Puzzle
Ramadan is Burnished Sunlight
Ala-udeen & The Magic Lamp (illustrated by the author)
The Crown of Creation (illustrated by the author)
Blood Songs
Down at the Deep End (with drawings by the author)
Next Life

THEATER / THE FLOATING LOTUS MAGIC OPERA COMPANY
The Walls Are Running Blood
Bliss Apocalypse

PROSE
Zen Rock Gardening
The Little Book of Zen

NEXT LIFE

POEMS

August 9, 2012 – February 12, 2013

DANIEL ABDAL-HAYY MOORE

THE ECSTATIC EXCHANGE

PHILADELPHIA

Next Life

Printed in the United States of America

For quotes any longer than those for critical articles and reviews, contact:
The Ecstatic Exchange,
6470 Morris Park Road, Philadelphia, PA 19151-2403
email: abdalhayy@danielmoorepoetry.com

First Edition
ISBN: 978-0-578-12022-5 (paper)
Published by The Ecstatic Exchange,
6470 Morris Park Road, Philadelphia, PA 19151-2403

Also available from The Ecstatic Exchange:
Knocking from Inside, poems by Tiel Aisha Ansari

The Divine Name calligraphy appearing on pages 9 and 2001 is adapted from a photograph taken by the author in the tomb of Shaykh Tijani, *raheemullah*, in Fes, Morocco.

Front cover collage by the author, back cover photograph by Malika Moore

بسم الله الرحمن الرحيم

DEDICATION

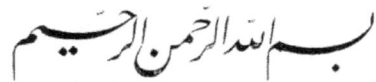

To
Shaykh ibn al-Habib (Allah be pleased)
(and the continuation of the Habibiyya)
Shaykh Bawa Muhaiyuddeen,
all shuyukh of instruction and ma'arifa
my wife Malika
(teacher of generosity and kindness)
and family,

and
Baji Tayyaba Khanum
of the unsounded depths

The earth is not bereft
of Light

CONTENTS

AUTHOR'S INTRODUCTION

(Bismillah er-Rahman er-Raheem)

There are among us luminous beings (and they really should be pictured with some kind of radiance around their heads or hearts, that as much as the ideologue materialists deny, these men and women exist even today and emit an unimpeachable luminosity) who maintain that what we might taste of the Garden of Paradise and what we might suffer of the Fire of Hell is right here in our present earthly and mortal existence as well. The imaginal truth of the Spiritual Path that points to the Next World *after* death is perhaps indisputable (however some might vigorously dispute it) but our lives, upon reflection, sometimes thrown overboard and barely making it to shore, sometimes buoyed up very high and slammed down very low and hard, are a living proof of the this-world tasting of the Next World experience. We might say, those of us who have embraced the after-death dimension of that undimensional existence, high and low, that "there" the intensification of both states or regions is mighty and magnificent and profound — and eternal — but that here and now gleams of both divisions can be felt, and even tasted.

It is in this vein, I think, that this book, *Next Life*, progressed from August of 2012 to February of 2013, in my usual rolling chronology along a single track of the writing of poems that are both autobiographical and beyond biography. My book just previous to this one, *Down at the Deep End*, serves as the initial volume blip in my output of this two-volume set, the first being the travails of cancer treatment, the summer of 2012, and recovery so marked, *alhamdulillah*, coming soon after. So this title has a kind of double meaning: *Next Life,* being the poems after *Deep End*, or a follow-up to a previous phase, but also an imperative, a command: *Next,* Life! For that is how it feels to come out of something dire, something even being a thin strand of smoke from the grave, that happily can turn to incense, but wakes us up in the very midst of hardship to the Grace and Miracle of existence, short or long, that God has given us in His unmysterious generosity. I say "unmysterious" because in clear sightedness that generosity is all around and within us at all times, and by the promise of true guided prophets, continues all the way to eternity and maybe beyond, if such could be. It's getting close to that divine breath that has such sweet perfume, available in the very trenches of misery and celebrated in the sweetly loosening heart-bindings of relief.

So the *Next Life* can be perhaps seen as the next domino to be extended from one phase or life-moment (that can be of tedious duration) to a following one, right after, a kind of open doorway out from that more stress-enclosed room to bright air and seemingly unlimited spaces, our own vision itself of it being of course the main limitation.

Over this period I noticed that my voice changed somewhat and my breathing stamina, due to the chemotherapy and intense thirty-five base-of-tongue-focused radiations I underwent, and during that time and since then (but in fact starting before) I've found myself writing shorter breath-units, ghazel-inspired self-contained couplets, that I can read out loud in a less earlier discursively long-breathed Projective energy. This also, curiously, is part of the *next life* I experienced coming out of the *deep end*, as it were. And I can only pray that they transmit some of the awe and joy and flushed out openness and perhaps greater simplicity of expression that I have experienced in God's Grace this past year, and with that continued Grace, in the adventurous and hopefully totally surprising but unknown and decreed years to come.

Seek the art of loosening knots.
Quick! Before your soul leaves your body.
Leave that nothing that seems like existence.
Seek the existence that seems like nothing.

— Rumi, (trans. Anvar & Twitty)

The face of Allah, the all-inclusive name Allah, embraces us defracted through the prism of each of our five senses as well as through our consciousness (thoughts, feelings, sense of self), inviting us to receive with gratitude the fragments of the name of Allah that come to us at each moment. When we start to gratefully receive these fragmentary embraces with each pore of the skin of our faces, our forearms, with our fingertips, with our palms; when we start to gratefully receive each sound that reaches our eardrums; when we start to gratefully receive each colored ray of light that strikes our eyes and optic nerves from whatever it is we see; when we start to gratefully receive the smells of the air that we inhale through our nostrils; when we start to gratefully receive each morsel of food and drop of drink that passes through our lips, embraces our tongues, and journeys down our throats; when we start to gratefully receive the Face of Allah, the name of Allah in these ways, the multi-sensory multi-dimensional symphony leaves us awestruck. All possible objects of our senses, including our sense of self and all we think and feel, are all orphans coming home, all heartlost lovers merging in this unity, all scattered notes coming together in this infinite symphony reaching its crescendo at each moment... *Allah... Allah.... Allah...*

May we gratefully receive all of this by sipping the drop of gratitude that Allah places at the tongue of our hearts,

— Shaykh 'Abd al-Haqq Godlas

Everyone has a succession of angels
in front of him and behind him,
guarding him by Allah's command.
Allah never changes a people's state
until they change what is in themselves.

— Qur'an 13:12 (Bewley translation)

HOW TO BEGIN

With rainbow puddles at our feet
and leaves the size of clouds?

Space is anywhere and everywhere
and we are onion-skin thin between it and

everything that passes
before us and

through us

Where is that bridge taking us
but one step ahead of us?

What zoom-lens brings it all
right before us?

Through a very small aperture
entire Paradises unfold

populated by preoccupied but
endlessly smiling faces

passing before us and through us

Our internal organs are
everyone's organs encased in our

momentary selves

Our liberated souls are
everyone's souls capable of

uttermost patience and
immediate ascensions

escaping from ourselves into
vertical territories horizontally

crowded with sky-dappled wings
migrating to creation's source

A wheel enters the picture
that crushes the asphalt it crosses

coming from anywhere and
going to anywhere

but its definite contact all along its
circumference with earth's solid road

is the buoyancy of our bodies
passing through air on our

way to everywhere

8/9

FULL-THROATED TREMOLO

How water wants to trickle through
and puts the pressure on

How light bursts into a place and
seeps through cracks

How energy can't be contained for long
in too small quarters

And how all this has a kind of
immortal flow

And how God's Name
resounds off itself and

multiplies while still
staying a single reed that

intones its ubiquitous melody as well as
crushes mountains

And how it comes through our
throats and arches out like

light or water

into the world that like
light and water

wants its energy to move
in a forward flow

and can barely be contained for all our
intensity of intentions to

do so
and how we also

like light and water forward
flow

His Name our tongues'
full-throated

tremolo

8/15

LIMBER LIMBS EXTENDING

Life comes in dressed in the usual
furbelows

I can't understand what's got into it
expecting us to take it at

face value

what with tiny zebra zigzags pouring out one side
and corpses pretending to walk out the other

hoping to pass for this or that
under a chiaroscuro sky

whistling every tune imaginable
honking horns at every crossroads

thinking if it just shows up at the
test site all will be well

while we all know the black lion behind the screen
takes no prisoners

Send it back to the starting point

See how it fares on its
own two feet

Swans float in the sky like
cutouts on sticks

and vines of verbiage are
already growing around our toes

but a deep silence may be the best
antidote after all

for a fresh heart
each beat gold

and loose and limber
limbs extending

8/15

LIONS' TEETH

Do not curse time, for time is Allah
— Hadith of the Prophet (peace of Allah be upon him)
" Time is Allah, because it is *inexorable*"
— Faqir Shakir Masoud

When Allah said *"six days"* He
meant six days but what does

"six days" mean?

When Allah created the teeth of the lion
He meant the teeth of the lion

but what do the teeth of the lion
mean as they

sink into our necks?

When streets turn with
us on them

where do we go?

How does air so
surround us and flow

through us and we
barely know

how it starts and stops
and we also

start and stop in it
as we go

If we see our planet from
out in space it's a

small glimmer in the dark

He created the seven heavens piled up
in six days

and it caused Him no hard work

Knowing God's love in a
matter of moments from its

inception to now is

our lives' arc
our lives' work

dying into Him
past this world's lion's teeth

here on His planet
breathing His air

as we disappear

8/17

BEYOND YOU

When you emerge out of the bowl of a
loud ringing bell

or slither from the pipes of your own
despair

or God opens the drapes of the day for you
onto broad sunlight

all the inadequate eloquence of
gratitude might

swarm around your throat like Monarchs
beating their thousand black and orange

wings to an ocean beat or at least some
beat beyond you

more in line with the origin of this
blessing upon you

able to better sing than you
yet from the pulse of your veins

a perfect replica of what is the
true you that is truly

beyond you

8/19

THE BODY INSIDE THE BODY

One ethereal palace inside the other

The body inside the body inside
the body

like gazelles leaping through flames

or the spot where we
focus our attention

past the high wall of ice and stars
pitch forks and rings of fire

Knocking on the outer gate
bringing commotion from within

the empty corridors and palazzos
echoing with footsteps

When the True Gate swings
open on its singing hinges

no one's on either side

And the silence of death
is a wind that hums to itself

crossing silver waters
to the farthest shore

the body inside the body inside
the body

where a small figure scattering
starlight increases its

wattage

to where we truly exist
unlike this world of

interpenetrating surfaces
dead ends and mourning

Entering one ethereal palace
inside another

reflected in the huge pond before it
in even huger moonlight

is the solitude through which
death enters us

and we're not afraid

the body inside the
body inside the body

where life is

like gazelles leaping
through flames

8/22

THE ALCHEMIST

The alchemist throws down petals
and roses appear

The saint throws down roses and
worlds appear

populated by saints

The world throws down petals
and black-cloaked figures in dry

rose shapes flow down empty
streets collecting them in sacks

A light appears like
petals slowly twisting and falling

and as they float past our eyes
our hearts appear as if for the

first time within our cognizant grasp
able to hear the first words of

babies in their wombs and the
last words of enlightened ones

whose dying is like simply
turning to look

in eternity's direction

where a rose-shaped world opens its
petals to let us enter

each one a different bell-note
pealing into the

silence
of a single sphere

8/25

TOTALITY OF SOUND

A trombone wanted to
stand on its bell and play a

prelude to angels

But angels are heralded with
trumpets whose high notes are so

high and distant and sweet it makes
birds shiver

The timpani wanted to join and began
vibrating their stretched skins

until the air was throbbing with
ascending low notes responded to by

dolphins in their interweaving pods

A celeste tried a few tinkly arpeggios
and space now scintillated to a

greater degree than before until
one by one the sky filled its

cone-shaped dome with a
fluttering multitude of angels

and in their midst Israfil with his
Israfilian horn at his lips

but they all held their fingers across their
lips to shush him from

blowing that note quite yet that would
bring all God's creation to its

knees in an ensemble of silence
equivalent to the totality of sound from

every sphere at once in a
reverberant crescendo

from which no gnat or elephant
pauper or prince

is exempt

8/25

PERPENDICULAR FLAME

I get up perpendicular
to where I was

just horizontal

Ducks paddling on a pond are
perpendicular to the pond

Even an airplane in flight is
essentially perpendicular to the

earth

I'll get up and go to the
bathroom and wash for the

Dawn Prayer

where I'll stand perpendicular
and prostrate as horizontally as possible

worshipping Allah Who is neither
perpendicular nor horizontal to us

neither in space nor out of space though
nearer to us than our jugular veins

and The Hearer to our calls

The Answerer to our prayers

Unseen in the seen
and seen in the Unseen

us alive in both geometrical positions
and a wide variety in between

projected out perpendicularly from our mothers
horizontal for a time

growing and stretching
until one day we get up

perpendicular and start
roaming earthly horizons

wholly subject to the
inexorable aspect of time

tall masts on ships
stalwart speeches at microphones

The slow dance of death
silhouetted against the moon

then enter the great horizontal
stillness of shady lagoons

and unruffled oceans
when their waves lie flat

and His Light falls down in a
fine silvery rain

our lives called out from their
non-dimensional glows

to resonate reflective
solar magnificence

to His ever
perpendicular Flame

8/29

AS WE GO

At the service of the unmultipliable
everything is multiplied

pouring in abundance inside and
outside us with golden

branches of delectable fruits all
sizes and flavors hanging within

reach should we
reach for them

and then within tasting should we
taste them

as each moment of Allah has its
particular flavor as we Oh so

rambunctiously roll along
tasting and rolling as we

go

rolling and tasting His most
magnificent abundance

as we go

8/30

LUMINOUS CUBE

There was a luminous cube
and inside it divine commotion

There was an ocean
and inside it a luminous cube

Teams of horses have tried to
pull apart the luminous cube

straining at every side at once

In the ocean the luminous cube
seems quite at home

every side under equal pressure from
the sea

Fires have been set upon it
great bombs fallen on it

It refuses to yield up its secrets

In the ocean the luminous cube
floats like a lackadaisical thing

nonchalantly swimming with the
urchins and the squid

But divine commotion is
divine commotion and

can't be kept down

which is why each of us is
startled awake by

God's Name and the
announcement of His

Presence among us in
signs and wonders

natural and supernatural
in the flowering orchards of the earth

as well as the fiery doings of
heaven and so far beyond

heaven after heaven
infinitely squared

until the sides of the
luminous cube become

transparent and we
see ourselves on both

sides of it at once
celebrating its

cubidity
and our

release from it and our flowing
into it

in God's air

9/1

GOD'S VOICE

To desire something
a number of fires have to be lit

and complicated sets of pulleys
set into motion and

levers and multitudinous mechanical
operations begun all with a fairly

loud whirring and squeaking of
wheels

That if for example all this takes
place at the ocean then the

noise of such desiring blocks out the
easygoing in and out slosh of

surf and overhead cries of gulls and
maybe children laughing as they

catch and throw beach balls

as if the whole crackling sound is
turned off as you

get up and go to the open air
hot dog stand or the

fresh fried jack fruit slices
as macaws pitch and

dive in the surrounding trees
until desire is

satisfied and you sit again looking
out at eternity among the

luminous shifting clouds
all still and quiet and the

whole oceanic symphony plays its
profounder music again

through your bones

Not to pass judgment on
desire *per se*

but to free its racket from
God's Voice being intermingled

and all else but that Voice
seeping back into the air from which it

came

and the radiant accompanying
lights on the horizon dazzlingly bright

as that scintillant crisp crystalline
Voice is clearly heard

9/5

AGLITTER

Flow of a bright green
paradoxical storm

out of a black sky down onto
prairies like a hundred whips held in

a thousand hands
engaging the moment in a

bison stampede to the four corners

where a forest of angels on foot
(except they have no feet)

await purification's
drops big as canon balls

to cover with their enormous wings
the black sky suddenly

aglitter with their rustling

9/6

MERCY

The beauty of Mercy is
greater than the Crystal of Light

God's Grace comes through the air
and finds us where we are

Wheelbarrows of putrid soil
dumped in the ravines of our *nafs*

cut through in an instant by one
ray of His Love from His

angle we don't suspect

I built a wall higher than the
Tower of Babel but a single

flutter of Mercy's breeze grazes my
cheek and the

wall falls all around me
at one stroke

Don't crowd the doorway with
self recriminations

but let Him in

No mountain in the glittering first
moments of dawn

is too high not to be smashed to
smithereens by His singular

Presence

Don't back away from the
bomb that's about to

explode in our hearts for His
space to prevail

and He inhabits no space

nor His nearness to overpower us
yet He inhabits neither

nearness nor farness but
both at once in His

multiple weather coil of Light
instant simplicity

A lake at the top of an
inaccessible height reflects His

invisible Face which is
everywhere

and each scintillant atom in the

air in us and around us
is that lake and that height

and none and all
and all and none

and without any motion
or motionlessness

He exits as all

And enters as One

9/8

ACROSS AN OCEAN OF SIGNIFICANT SIZE

Across an ocean of significant size
comes a voice of significance

with veils of purple droplets
shielding it from view

and foam-lipped waves curling towards it
underneath

"Shed your shoes
that your feet feel earth's
insubstantial swiftness
underneath"

A horn of light
angles down from dawn

its blast a simple scintillation
over the black mass of
ocean underneath

"The body's glow
surrounds soul's golden
bar of God's volition
airier than air"

It's not anger that keeps the waves'
motion in the

black ocean underneath

but love's machinations that
gnash their passionate
teeth

Darkness itself now
visible in total
silence speaks

"We toss and turn you
higher and lower until you
recognize Who's indivisibly
in charge above and
underneath

atom by atom
heartbeating forward in
time without

cease"

9/13

A SEA OF STARS

A broken jug on a table full of
broken jugs

A rooster the size of a small horse

A house built with no
doors or windows

Death that walks below the
horizon of a hill

A sound that hovers in
air for three days

A side of light that can be
sliced like steaks and

served on plates

The six billion or so of earth's
population each with a full size

mirror that reflects
God's Face

Ocean water the color of
rainbows and rainbows on

everything

Swans dyed pink

A game so hard to play
no one wins

Water so hard to cross
no one comes back

A song so hard to sing
we all stay silent

its melody sweet its words
omnivorous its impact

the next life
made suddenly real

If I go away now
I'll wonder if I've ever been here

Having been here
I wonder if I'll ever return

Returning is all we seem to do
moment to moment after

inhabiting spaces of unconsciousness

where the spheres reside
and the outermost planets

and we can't go there
except in the holy heart

nor expect anything but the
terrors of the void

unless it be the golden bath of
divine love

entitled to each of us
knowingly or not

before the corral is shut
on a moonlit midnight

under a sea of stars

9/14

STILL SCATTERING

Most of our houses block us from
seeing the stars that much

in the sense that a coyote's house
doesn't

or a vulture's
if they happen to look

and though the heavens with all their
unsubtle activity stretch not only

above us but extend on and on more than
any distance from us

and are worthy of our
constant awe and continual

contemplation yet we generally
take it for granted that they're

there and we're here
diminuendo'd by their vastness and

as squinty-eyed as a rhinoceros by our
near-sightedness in their regard

with those fuzzy little lights say

up there in their incomprehensible

gazillions coming to birth or
extinguishing themselves like

so many sparks on an otherwise
smooth ebony honeycombed dimensional

surface without the
accoutrements at least in our rational

world of dragons or griffins
cavorting freely in the endless

implacable swirl

echoless and beyond the human
a vastness that just keeps going

out and out past every
Nirvana and Valhalla every

Paradise or otherwise populated
world both proto-and-post-

physical that we might
visit if we wished in person

as Ibn 'Arabi did in his most
fluid being by just a

flip of his innermost switch
with Allah's and His beloved

Prophet's *(peace be upon him)*
help and permission

and came back with the
news of his starry and

interplanetary adventure

that stardust of his still scattering
everywhere around us

9/15

THE DAY OF PLEASURE

The day of pleasure's arrived!
Rivers are running with wine

Polar bears and gazelle
romp together on the greensward

those huge rolling lopes of bear
and bamboo-like leaps of gazelle

against a topaz sky turned
turquoise at its edges

a golden radiant glow pulsing endlessly
at its center

We see in each other's eyes
God's Names in perfect script

by the most exquisite calligraphers
scratching with nothing but light

Half the earth slopes away from us
while the other half ascends

halfway to heaven

Cornstalks grow higher than clouds
their bronze tassels ringing like bells

We're not far now from eternity in a wink
and the meandering valleys from there onward

Since it's already begun we
don't have to be convinced of its existence

Even the taste of snow in the air
won't deter us

Every mode of transport to there's
been set in motion

Skylarks make horizontal circles
above our heads

Death wears a red cloak
and won't stop dancing

We'll slip past it into the night
unseen

Death won't notice our departure
among the general evanescence

and we won't notice it either
so utterly drunk on sky's moonlight

9/16

A MORTAL BODY

Getting out of a mortal body is hard

especially if you've got nowhere to go

9/20

GOD'S FLOW

I've gotten all bony
before I'm all bones

and more angular now to
earthly reality

I'm skinnier now
than before I got sick

What I've lost in weight
I've gained in space

"Walk lightly on earth"
God says in Qur'an

We get lighter and lighter
the more we go

until finally we weigh
nothing at all

but a finer flow
within God's flow

9/27

MAGNIFICENCE

Magnificence can't be bought or sold

However extravagant a piece of
jewelry or a house in Monaco

only jagged dust flakes next to
Allah's Magnificence

in big and small things
microscopic or atomic

wave after wave of it pours direct
from magnificent Source jostling even

Allah's own magnificent things aside for His
immeasurable Magnificence

to pour forth

Take a rock for example
an ugly gray rock

on a trail deep in a woods
in the near-dark of day

sitting there
nondescript

doesn't fit against
anything else to make a more

formidable rock

hardscrabble
unique

Now I'm looking down at it
from my standpoint

and it may be looking at
me from its

but how we both got here
at this moment

it from untold millennia
me from my seventy-two years

it kicked by whatever to wherever
of no use to anyone

in the middle of a path going
somewhere

before the sun slips around
below the horizon

leaving us both in the dark
and the stars come out

one or two rays landing on us
me and the rock

eye to eye as it were
me passing on

that funny-shaped bit of things
commanding the entire

universe
from its royal

perch

submitting and
immobile

existent in all its
divine magnificence

9/28

DOVES

1

Doves know the direction they
need to turn

even in the midst of a
yellow sky

and when they turn the whole earth
pitches sideways

to them and they aren't
confused nor do they

conceive there's no branch or
windowsill to return to

and the yellow sky might turn
more golden or it might turn blue

but these genius doves
fly through it to where they

need to go and when they get there

coo in warbling harmonies
from whatever it is that

inspires them to coo so
warblingly

2

Dove in the air already
where I like to get to

when I've taken a run for it
to get the poem started

after the dove's talking feather
fallen from the sky

stands on its quill before me
and slowly line by line and

feather by feather
a dove's constructed

before me

transparent as the air itself
ready to fly without me

already in mid-flight
even before we've spotted each other

and I catch it in
full flight within me

catch you in full flight *O dove*
God's Light diving and dipping

fitting the air
like a white velvet

glove

9/29

SUGAR AND SALT

A temple was built in a
spoonful of salt

a mausoleum in a bowlful of
sugar

The air sparkled and shone with an
unnatural splendor

Harps played from the four corners

The temple rose into crystalline spires
the mausoleum expanded horizontally

Each refracted spheres of light
into themselves

Harp music covered them over with
webs of incandescence

All but them in negative space became
lacquered darkness

They continued to grow exponentially
as only crystals grow

salt and sugar
taller and wider

The only animals interested
were the legless slitherers

A few parrots landed on roofs and
flew away

A door opens in all this
through which we may

walk onto hillsides of rolling
grass and lush orchards

odors in the golden air like
intimations of other worlds

10/1

THE BEAUTY OF THE FACE

The beauty of the face is in
the humility of the heart

Straw in which a colt is born
radiant as a saint

Somehow the barn window
lets in all the light

Its beam slants down and
touches us

our limbs supple and still

Layers of peacefulness from our
heart's pulse upward

enough to build a world

A pin drop of arrogance
ruins it

Stand beside yourself
and say nothing

Except to Him who never and
will never betray your golden solitude

A colt's first wobbly steps
looking for the milk of its mother

A lone dust-filled wind blows
banging the barn doors open

on a landscape where
God's breath has irradiated

all the things of the world
that lie sleepily inside your face

The long morning has
exhausted us

All of time leading up to this
moment that shatters

into a billion light blots

where you can see
the heart that engulfs you

10/9

THE DRUNK

The foot that kicks the rock
connected to the leg of the

mind that thinks it

is like elixir from the Unseen
now seen and tasted by the tongue

of the drunk who drinks it

10/11

DARK AS LIGHT AS DARKNESS ITSELF

The dark road is pretzel-shaped
and leads us to our hearts

The universe itself is shaped like a
ring on the fringe of flying space

dazzling all the farthest stars in its glory

and the planets circulate in a
slow waltz

in time to our pulse

If our eyes are open
giraffes of light lope across fields of

nothingness

Nobody son of Nobody has already
been here and left a

trail of light winding around the

first tree that is the
last tree

If we shout loud enough
silence will ring its bells

If we dive deep down enough into
silence its reverberations will

lead us to our first home
and our last home will open its

doors as wide as all space itself
shaped like an arc of darkness

across God's Throne
shaped somewhere between the

Inconceivable and the inconceivably
Inconceivable

Whose love filters unceasingly down
through light in the shape of

ourselves
gone in a wink into

darkness' light as
dark as lightness itself

10/13

THE NATURE OF THINGS

A boat by its nature
floats on top of water by its

nature that would
drown the boat if it weren't

built to keep it from drowning

A house by its
nature is built to keep out the

elements that by their
nature would overcome and

infiltrate the house if its
roof and walls weren't built to

keep them out and enable the
house's inhabitants to be

warm and dry inside even if
blizzards and downpours rage

for days outside

10/15

I'M SLEEPING IN THIS GREAT BODY

I'm sleeping in this great body on the
sofa under the lamplight

This great body that holds within it
constant painless organic procedures

transforming food into blood cells and energy and
shucking the excess waste into suitable labyrinths

and the heart like a giant engine in this
huge Titanic of a body I'm sleeping in

on the sofa under the lamplight
in a mist of internal consciousness

while covered with a light blanket
and watched by our cat under the

round living room table

this mythic giant of chemical perfection
this living alchemical beaker God's

fashioned me to live in like a
primitive barge from birth to death with all the

modern conveniences of lungs and liver and
kidneys and brain each with its

form and function generally intact and
surprisingly efficient for their seventy-two years

and living in a perfect world of water faucets and
grocery stores oak and maple forests and

steam heating
in this body whose legs I extend out over the

Grand Canyon in an evening's chill
and whose hands I place across my

chest in reverent sleep
knowing it's all going perfectly as

planned each perfect drop of life
in this Titanic of a body

dripping through me
from end to end

10/16

O MY DEATHS! O MY BIRTHS!

But *O my deaths!*
O my births!

Woodchuck on the opposite tree
felling a giant to fall

down on me
his flat tail slaps the water and

makes a great sound
that reverberates the forest into a

leaf that fits my hand so perfectly

Deaths out of me through the
pores of me

across black waters

Births proficient equally

Spring coiled deep inside impending
winter's death canoe

watertight for travel through
all the ones of

birth and death reflected in each
flake of snow that falls

Handsprings over the
broken rocks and waterfalls

O births O deaths of me
leaving dead leaves in the prostrate

shapes of me

No cell of us that does not know
eternity

10/20

(Note: I made a mistake thinking a woodchuck was another name for a beaver. It's not: it's a kind of groundhog. If a woodchuck could chuck wood, it *might* be a beaver.)

SOME ADAGES

If you have a lot
give some of it away

If you have nothing
give it *all* away

A blue rose on a red rosebush
is a prize to blue rose fanciers

a bane to red rose purists

The lion that lays down with a
lamb is one thing

the lion that curls its tail
protectively around a lamb another

Flame that's afraid of water and
won't go near it is

flame that remains flame

Flame that dives into the
water and is extinguished

enters God's domain

A snake ate its tail and
swallowed itself

Eternity is a möbius strip
that swallows itself and

gives birth each moment

What is it that keeps
passing before our eyes

God's projections on a
blank screen

multifarious in the zillions
whose origin is a single Light

Ours the laughter
and weeping at gravesides

under weeping willows
who may actually be laughing

There's no end to it
when we stop

it keeps going
under divine decree

in His most able hands

When we step off the carousel
the circular procession of

mute wooden animals
waits

10/28

IF YOU POUR ALL THE SALT

If you pour all the salt in the
world on your head will you be

humble?

If you slant the beams of all the
lighthouses on the crags of your

thoughts will light enter their
cracks?

Can our hearts leap out of our
bodies and dance with the stars?

Since childhood you've failed to
spot the white deer standing in the

snow so still no flake moves
and the sky pings a

silver silence longer and
wider than death itself

If a wind blows will your body
quail or stiffen in

resistance?

Out of a stubborn stance no song
flows

A heart harder than granite
engenders no rose

10/31

SOME COMPARISONS

The faith and persistence of a gambler
compared with that

waterfall over there

The speed and width and evanescence of a
runaway locomotive down a track

and the thought that just disappeared
from my head forever

A canary's festive song in its cage
at the first crack of sunlight

and this heart of ours always on the
lookout for tears of joy and

tears of heartbreak

This moment we're all in everyone of
us the cat and the moth included

and clouds dispersing from a sharp
mountain peak among the Matterhorn

range aglitter with impermanence

These songs that come to us
enticed into daylight at just the

tiniest crack in space whose
door just a tiny bit opens

and floods of tsunami waters
awaiting God's signal to rise up and

pour their uttermost tonnage through
village and city rural

outpost and downtown Manhattan

keeping us on our toes to remember to
sing and stay on our toes in

all kinds of weather

in the atmospheres of transformation
whose ever-shifting punctuality of divine

clockwork may be

all we can depend on
at last

11/1

WITH MY FEET

With my feet still firmly in all my
past lives

past present future too
future growing already into past

I sit fastened now to none and
neither and yet

them all and others I
know not now though yet might

sprout from the so-called other three

and the rose trellis growing outside my
door in night's pitch dark

and a vague purplish light
converging around all three

as they pertain to me
in extensions with their accompanying

voices and memory shufflings
even the recollection at this

moment of my future worlds

that could shoot anywhere but
won't they'll go where all the

others went
on Allah's fine feathered four-

dimensional globe of it all
that from this vantage right now

with some jaggedy film clips running
hither and skelter helter and yon

in browns and mauves and pale
Technicolors with blurry sounds

of doors creaking and faces speaking

is God's Light fanned in
all dimensions at once

being perfectly spread on each of their
bubbly horizons

that I hold in my heart

the way a child holds the strings
of different heliums

and His Divine Face reflects finally
in a heavenly lake

suspended in
indefinite space

and the details of all three
entirely effaced

11/2

THE STARS TELL A DIFFERENT STORY

The stars tell a different story
since their great distances from us

give them a wider perspective
and a far longer sense of time

out there in space

And though they are just like us in their
thusness their hard rockiness their

passionate fieriness or complete gasiness

still perspective is everything and you
can't say they don't have that in

spades

Plus from our earthly perspective
though baseless from one

point of view their distance puts them in
greater proximity to God's

natural dimension
incomprehensible vastness barely

approachable awesomeness even when
compared to jugular nearness

even when considered along with the
angels circulating in our blood

Still the stars tell a different story
where history so momentous to us

is this tiny pinpoint in nothingness
where barely anything's taken place

Black Plague civil wars hurricanes
yet in the middle of it all we

can't be faulted for taking it so
dramatically you know the

grief and bother of it
the discomforts of the

inexorableness of time's ravages
time's sometimes too subtle

miracles to notice how truly
miraculous they are

from the perspective of the stars

and how we shine in every
God space we're in

in the very midst of the too
muchness of it all the

overwhelmingness that curves over us
its astonishing waves

our curious ability to
stand up in all of it

even as it's happening
and usually come out of it with

stories to tell
even though and generally we have the

feeling during the telling itself
that the stars tell a

different story
a little closer perhaps

to God's

11/3

MY DAUGHTER'S IN LABOR

My daughter's in labor far away
and tigers have come down

to watch her and watch over her
the earth coming up to lick her heels

the waters in Tomales Bay
listening to her cries

Stars configure their configurations
over her

and sheep sway in the night from
the music they feel from their

hooves upward

She's holding both sides of the
universe together as her

first child pokes out as slowly as it
can into the colder world outside her

waiting to warm it at its breast
which is her own breasts grown

milkier than the Milky Way itself
in which we ride

birthing and dying
bright rainbow streaks against black

The silhouette of other animals
coming near

to watch over her in her labor

until the stars above her
form a siphon and a mirror

to draw the incarnated soul out
and be reflected now forever

everywhere it goes
in God's perfect Wisdom

11/4 (2 a.m.)

DEATH'S TREE

I always thought death was like
walking into the inside of a

great tree
and the tree closing around you

and the tree continuing to grow
with you inside it

and the horizon expanding horizontally
an expanse wider than anyone's

field of vision
with a snow owl or two

swooping across it
gray fog and tundra

mixing into one
that goes on indefinitely

And it's not really goodbye to
all we loved in the world so much as

turning to face in another direction
than any degrees between the

cardinal points we're born into

Echoes from inside the tree
pouring out into space from the

death side
a new space we'd never seen before

as green and fertile as any
earth space we'd seen and loved

but now the tree growing with us inside it
putting out its usual

seasonal leaves

11/6

VOICES ON THE AIRWAVES

The time for thought is over —
Hold to the sides of the golden boat

The trees that pass you
can't be counted

Voices on the airwaves are a
scramble of intelligent noise

A horn is sounded from a
turquoise hill

A sheep is *baaing* before it
turns to silver

Thought's just come to a
halt in open space

Stutters before magnificence
with its jaw dropped

Its eyes are ours but its
mind is elsewhere

Structurally round then
structurally unsound

Allah greater than
absolutely everything

Name each thing before it
floats away

Our prerogative is naming
His prerogative is Light

The patchwork is our lives
His is the whole quilt

Hold to the sides of the golden
boat that dissolves in water

Where we're going demands
utter silence and a single word

Opening and closing are a
matter of degree

Being here is beyond such
mechanical operations

The time for thought has
come and gone

as the gong resounds

A trickle of water is an
ocean to an ant

A slave who throws his
master overboard becomes a

slave to that drowning

In the golden boat our
hearts become smaller than a

hair that contains every
universe known to God alone

The whinny of a horse
wakes us

and we see we're
on the other side

a tremendous space opening
and there's no one here

11/9

COUNTRY COLD

"In country cold
with small green frogs

clinging to a window
their throats warbling"

— begins a poem that can't be
properly concluded

just as anywhere anytime
the poem begins long before us

and extends way past us —

Visiting our daughter and her
two-week old baby Amadine

curled up in their California country cabin
before wood stove fire

glowing in its black iron

Autumn rain pelting down around us
(strange drops of bright nosebleed in my

sink in the morning)

The utter comfort of a huge new bed
with sumptuous coverlet

the almost hissing of the
silence all around us

Crisp country cold
like white light

outlining us

11/16

THE SPARKLE OF ANGELS

He read one line:
"The sparkle of angels comes from the

tips of their wings"

and the universe pulled back its forehead
and showed him its

innermost heart

He was walking
and had nowhere else to go

He was sitting and there was
nowhere else to walk to

He was breathing
and he had no death left

Wherever he looked
God completely surrounded him

Wherever he went
there was nowhere left behind

What was spoken to him
spoke through him

One day there was a match that
lit by itself

and burned the place down

What was left became the
nothingness that always was

The sound of the river is
river enough for most of us

When he opened his mouth there was
nothing but river for the rest of us

It's not enough to be ourselves
we must be bereft of ourselves

to see God

To the left of ourselves
is the rest of ourselves —

Then he closed the book and
went back to work

dead to the world
no longer left to himself

11/18

IN THE DREAM

In the dream there was a crowd of us
moving slowly forward everyone

in *djallabas* mostly
white or gray woolen ones

— all men —

and as I was walking with the
others I felt someone behind me

adjusting the folds of the hood down at my
back and carefully patting the

corners in place and flattening the
point downward

and I saw it was Shaykh Abdal Qadir
with his long careful fingers

and he said to me behind me as we
walked

*"Once you get it right it's right
forever"*

and we continued forward with the
crowd and I moved ahead and it seemed

I could sense who I was in his eyes for a
moment as someone very young but

on my own now and finished
impeccably turned out

moving forward in the crowd

Upon relating the dream to my wife Malika
she said it was because

he had indelibly instilled love of the
Prophet Muhammad in us *(salla 'llahu*

alayhi wa sallam) that once established
is never lost

and that is
true

11/18

WHAT IF ALL THE MIRACULOUS

What if all the miraculous
aspects of existence were just a

shill to get us *inside* the tent

Crystalline lights of winter
kaleidoscopic spectral rainbows

inside each flake
waterfalls frozen into

cathedrals of glass

Serendipitous meetings in
crowds with the one who

turns out to be the perfect mate
with all the honking and

hullabaloo but inside a circle of eternal serenity
where this wedding takes place

Words tumbling out of the Master's
mouth whose eyes are like twin

green pastures where purest white
horses graze

and whose words turn out to be not only
prophetic but exactly and precisely

true

Miracles that abound in Amazonian
varieties of plant and creature

lemur and pharmacopeia of healing herbs and
hallucinatorily gorgeous bright plumaged

birds

Invisible visitations and the very
perfect rotations of earth around the

heartbeating sun
our balanced placement in this

splashed universe of stars

What if everything we could enumerate
even more subtle than the

last
were all just an enticement

to get us face to face with the

Master of miracles Exhaler of
Light Sender of wonders

unceasingly and ever-productively

Merciful between every moment however
miniscule conceived of and tasted

all just a trick to get us
into His tent

no intermediary

face to Face?

11/19

THREE DREAMS

1

In the first dream we were in a kind of large
institution or college and we were

called together to form lines as if to do the
prayer and I was in a second or third line

near the right-hand side one boy from the
end and boys were

running into line when I heard the
voice of the headmistress

who began reading from *Winnie the Pooh*
which she read from for it seemed a

very long time
finally saying *"Where's Daniel Moore?"*

as I was meant to receive the book she was
reading from as an award

It was handed down the line to me and I was
a bit embarrassed and put it

face down in front of me on a kind of
shelf that appeared and the boy

next to me said *"Have you read it?"*
And I replied somewhat archly

"Yes when I was ten!" but he seemed to think
it was quite an honor

Later the headmistress was brought out in a kind of
litter all wrapped up as if she were ill

I went to her
a youngish woman with black hair

Indian or Pakistani lying on her side
and I bent down and asked if she was

alright
she said no that she felt ill

I felt her forehead which was
feverish and

told her so

2

In the second dream I was the poet in
residence in a very upscale Indian shop that sold

gorgeous antiques and jars and various
items from India

I was in the back of the shop among a
huge display of bamboo flutes

I found a small one and began
playing a beautiful simple tune

then gathered about ten of different sizes to
take home with me

The proprietor's partner came along and said
"Time to go

we can't just do poetry all day"
and I suddenly thought I shouldn't

take the flutes at all

A while later when we were leaving I noticed
he'd put them all in a reddish

duffel bag to I assumed
take with him

3

In the third dream
a Pakistani friend and I were

sitting in a restaurant as guests or it
could have been just one room in a

private home and we were being
treated to a special meal

The room was painted bright blood red with
blue or green trim and although I

can't recall the meal it was many courses
each sumptuous and delicious

At the end we were standing outside the
room and I was talking to our

hostess amd her husband was
standing back by the door in a blur

I was thanking her and noting she was
Pakistani I mentioned so was my

friend

While we were talking a few men in overalls had come
into the room we were just in and

began painting the walls a very strong dark
cobalt blue

11/19

VIVID STEREO

Then there's that sense in the country

that space is rushing by —

that sound of it like a

rushing river in vivid stereo

call it *wind-in-the-trees*

space itself like a river everywhere

with a rushing current

in all vastness around us

11/20

ANYWHERE OTHER THAN

Anywhere other than
where you are

is nowhere

Neither fearing the Fire
nor desiring the Garden

only *Allah*

and again

Allah

---

and again

Allah

11/21

THE ENERGY WE EXPEND

The energy we expend
hacking through our daily trough

if it were filled with star sparks
might illuminate our slightest action

each gesture an energy transmitter
from the glittering of our eyes

to the whale-like modulations of our
vocal chords diving down into the

deeps

from pole to pole of the earth on its
tilted axis

perfect in its spatial placement
for meaning to come pouring through us

and spreading like a surf around us
fuzz of bubbles bursting in the

air

No meaning without form
until all form dissolves

when all is only meaning
nakedly pressed against

our hearts
in love

11/22

AND HOW THE BODY HEALS ITSELF

And how the body heals itself
in such a comparatively short time

My own after 3 chemos and 35 radiations
enough to burn down a small village

with just a bit of thickening from
scar tissue at my throat and

tingling in fingertips and left foot

And my daughter's healing but still
sore just three weeks after

delivering a seven pound baby girl perfect
to the tips of her ears and toes

out of her body

And if I had to deliver a baby that way
I know I'd say more than just *"ouch"*

So the whole business of birth is
nothing short of cataclysmically miraculous

and that she survives and loves the
child and suckles her immediately proves

my point even more sublimely

That the dear body gets bullet-holed
battered and bruised and

blown up bounced bulldozed ballyhoo'd
and bounced *(did I already say "bounced"?)* and still

bounces back to nearly normal again for a
few more rounds in the mortal

ring whose Ringmaster wreathed in
cloud with celestial whistle keeps things

wrangling in tough sweetness muscle by
muscle and atom by atom atop Old

Smokey on hillside and plain and we
shepherd ourselves and others with

life and limb to the edges and then to the absolute
middle again a strange

godly light around all of us
reflective of God's Light

shone directly
upon us

11/22

IRON OF THE CLANK

The iron of the clank
of the shank that

chugs around the
track locomotive

clang of bell
crack of pistons

listening to the ping
deep in the churlish

bowels of the hot iron
well of the firewall

feeding its fall
pell mell to the

bell's clang as it
chugs around the track

clank of iron and shrill
shank locomotive

fiery as hell

around and around the dull
track

well done
done well

there and back

11/27

RADIOLARIA

To sort through the various
radiolaria

all microscopic or sub-microscopic
luminous snowflake organisms

elusively detailed to the tiniest symmetrical filaments
in their painstaking

portraits by Darwin contemporary
Ernst Haekel drawn with

staggering precision before
hi-tech means of so doing

To see them at all
by only a handful of us

yet witnessed and commented on by
awed eye-witnesses whose

hearts are now imprinted with these
ectoplasmic presences

and who really can't put into adequate
words what they've seen

and to then think of all the

further luminous wonders left

unseen whose number no doubt far
outnumbers the seen ones

through electro-magnetic microscopes
everything so utterly subatomic seemingly

created with aesthetic rigor and
truly mind-boggling beauty of

perfection bacterial ballerinas atomic
architectural structures seen from any angle

projected molecules from an infant's fingernail
onto a giant screen

then imaginatively ferried forwards or
backwards through our

universe collapsing all the
light years as best we can to only a

few seconds or minutes apart for the
benefit of our terrestrial view

where we'd see the same magnificent
principles at play throughout

as far as the eye could see and the
heart contemplate

all before it blinks out in a
fine exhalation more ecstatically

luminous than all the rest until the
next inhalation by us or not by us

but by the unbroken chain of living
continuation in His sight

and our sight and sound barrier crossed
into the next world of even more

extravagant wonders

11/28

COMMUNING WITH ANGELIC ORDERS

On December Eighteenth I have a
surgery to remove the

last lymph lump from my neck

If it endangers my voice should I choose
an Electrolarynx artificial voice box

or be mute?

Sayyedina Zakariyya *(peace be upon him)*
stood outside the temple for three days

and spoke to people with
hand gestures alone to tell of

his wife's pregnancy with John the Baptist
"Glorify at dawn and evening!"

momentous and earthshaking news

Would I have anything more of the
moment to say

or would God be silencing me for His own
intimate conversation?

To live in a dimension of speechlessness

forevermore?

I almost desire it
though fear its limitations

communing with angelic orders
my cries unheard

12/4

DIFFERENT ALTITUDES

1

This world is *a sheath inside a*
sheath inside a sheath

each one the single
Face of God

At the tops of pine trees
cones mature to be

prickly hand grenades of
potential pines

tiny seeds as fragile as
eyelashes

becoming giant gnarled wooden lungs no
bear can fell

in a spyglass held
to a pirate's eye

in a glimmer of sunlight
as the sun falls

and night's axe thuds
to the ground

and the pirate sails on
his rendezvous forestalled

and the next bay
curving to his charms

among the tall ships

held in the hands of
fortuitous angels

whose errands have taken them
to a ragged continental shore

of this planet held in space
the way a spinning top suspends

between two nothingnesses
atop an endless void

packed to the stars with
sentient being

whose endlessness is God's Face
All-Seeing

2

This airplane is hitting some
lovely high notes

above the moaning
mantra of its motor

Why this plane doesn't fall
I can't tell

but Allah has His way with
physics

and on it sails

everyone inside it particularly
involved with inner pictures

still or moving as they may
elegant or sordid

who can tell
a sheath inside a sheath inside

a sheath
in which we dwell

opening out in timelessness
from time to time

until our selves are open
like light bursts from a

shell on a beach
and all the oceans swell from it

into a single pearl
reflecting all the light the

sun can send it
like water

underfoot and under-valued
gushing from a well

3

"I've tried different altitudes"
says the pilot like a Sufi saint to the passengers

apologizing for the really tumultuous turbulence

some passengers continuing to read or
glued to their iPads

Others of us saying our prayers

This butterfly balsa of fluttering wings and
silent prayers tossed on the airwaves like

scattered thoughts or
irregular heartbeats

in the black night just after
sunset flashed the horizon with a

volcanic blaze of gorgeous fire

we eventually calmed to a
more regular pitch

God's smoother altitudes
soothing us home

12/5

EACH MOMENT'S DANCES

The solid granite wall that encloses
the ephemeral sphere of spider web laciness

is made up entirely of shadows
and around that wall are

shadows of shadows that enclose that
wall

and extending outward are shadows upon
shadows to each cardinal point

and the farther each one reaches
the brighter the sphere inside shines

more incandescently and dimensionlessly
vast

so that as walls upon walls multiply
so does the girth of the ephemeral sphere

in size and brightness
and anyone who sees it is absorbed into it

as denser and darker shadows
reach all the way to the farthermost

horizons and the sphere nearly engulfs

the entirety of existence in every dimension
and its witnesses now are looking

out from within it

each face of subtlest substance
whose eyes are pure in their

seeing each moment's dances

in the scattering long-wing'd flying

birds of their glances

12/7

IN SLEEP

In sleep I take the position of
one of the Civil War dead

or an embryo curled up inside the womb

or a lizard sunning itself on an Arabian
desert dune

unconscious really of my position
but aligned with all these in the

parallelism of sheer existence

the sinking of a dolphin to sleep for a few
seconds near the bottom

or a fox in her den before daybreak
surrounded by cubs

or even in the center of the Amazon
a flowering plant that actually

wakes up and opens its waxy fronds
from some deep sleep

glorious on its black stem

and a continent of sleepers wakes up
inside us after its full variety of

nocturnal adventurers flying in stasis

fully submitting to God's good pleasure
as we sleep

12/8

EACH SECOND'S FALL

A sparrow sings
and other sparrows follow

An ant wobbles
across a scented path

A horse whinnies
and others from their stalls

Allah leads us
to where our hearts respond

It's not training
that teaches bees their dance steps

A river flows
where ditches make a path

A tree grows
between the other trees

Allah sends us
clear directions home

An infant opens
eyes for the first time

A flower opens
petals at the right season

When a door knocks
you sing out *"Come in!"*

God takes us completely
through the heart of darkness

The other side
has a far more breathable air

Shadows fade
around burning daylight

Cows wend
their way through the homeward gate

A shooting star
seems to be scorching heaven

Allah's peace
flows through our outstretched limbs

Allah's promise
comes true each second's

fall

12/9

COMPASSIONATE ZONE

Streaks of color in the sky
can it be the blood of angels?

The sky itself
can it be the breath of God?

In the underbrush a noise
a something's there

cleaning house?

The four or five or more
dimensions

a ghost's body
giving birth to life?

We travel to the cardinal points
then are we anywhere

but at our starting point?

Questions come
and are themselves the answers

A Cyclops or unicorn
as easily as an ant?

Staring into the air
are we gazing at

God's aquarium?

Loving each other to the bone
are we loving any

other than God?

You're seventy-two Abdal-Hayy
yet you're still a child

Still at sea
any closer to the shore?

Or is the sea the answer?

Love comes in a puddle
as well as a pillow

Do you breathe it in
and exhale its

compassionate zone?

12/11

BED FOR THE NIGHT

We make our bed
for sleep every night

Dunes will cover us
Earth is our lover

pull back the covers and
add a blanket

Clouds float above us
come together and drift apart

throw the day pillows
behind the bedstead

Will angels visit us in the
middle of our sleep?

A narrow bed
fit for sainthood

With all our faults we're
wrapped in our bedclothes

Sheets of light almost
visibly surround us

Winding sheets wait for us
like the spirals of snail shells

Where on this wide earth does our
narrow bed stand?

God's oceans all around us
God's air in our lungs

12/14

RIGHT NECK DISSECTION

I'm going to slaughter
Pull my head back
Slit with a knife
Doctor Cut-Throat

What'll he find?
Pieces of eight?
Radiant tissue?
Meat-colored fluff?

How will it be?
Angels proceeding?
Song burst forth
From the wide-mouthed opening?

All for the good
French Revolution
Partial guillotine
To bring me to health?

Lord Sayyedina Ibrahim
Be with me now
We all go to slaughter
For the Glory of God

12/16

AT MOMENTOUS TIMES

1

At momentous times in our lives
do we look out the window of our train

as it crosses the Alps?

Bore a hole from the inside through the
slats of the Trojan Horse to get a

better view?

Canoe down the Danube in a
frail birch bark canoe?

At momentous times such as these
are the scrolls unrolled from the

backs of our heads
saved from the fire that trashed the

library of Alexandria so fast
all that remained was

ash?

Do we wet our lips for a veil of high oratory?
Search through our pockets for the

aphorism jotted down on a cashier's receipt?
Listen more intently to the car mechanic's analysis

for his true beating heart
and most trustworthy intonation?

Do we descend a rope into our own well
to excavate relics or taste the darkest and

deepest water?

Cross the veldt when the
largest ibexes absentmindedly graze?

Rainbows pop up on all the horizons
where sudden silhouettes of secondary school girls

dance in their triangular skirts

It's time to pour our hearts out
at this most momentous of moments

singing to a sea of silver crests under
barest moonlight

extending its white for miles and miles
over the water's tumult

There's nothing like it
except the next crisis

whose moment is already
gearing up for its

eternal return

So that no matter what hat of
rainwater and roses we wear

times of ease and times of
disease are sure to come

the bull's breath already fogging our
eyes and the crowd

already hushed

2

Ah — good!
God's command's come due

White sheep stream through a gate
A ship's prow pierces the fog

A surgeon approaches with his knife

Somewhere there's celebration
ceilings of roses lower

closer to hand
floors ripple as we go

A multi-painted horse of
kaleidoscope hues walks in

Something new in its eyes never seen before
in horses

Buildings disappear and the
land's configuration in ancient times

appears

The command falls due with a ping
like silver spoons hitting trays

like tree tops bursting through snow
or whales breaching

their water spray falling back on the
waves below

Now my moment meets God's moment
though they're really only one

intricate moment engulfing with its wings
each feather's tooth-zipper distinct

and clear

an upending of what's been unseen
a pressing from what's been against

against what's not been
against but now

in full view is
suddenly here

is here

12/17

DIMENSIONAL HEART DIMENSIONAL THINKING

for James Daniero, MD

A beached whale is like a
planet come to die

Its bulk is so improbable
and that it looks through

whale eyes such an
unimaginable miracle!

If we forget the beauty of our origins
we forget the majesty of our end

That one time giants plodded and
plowed through the grasslands and

waters of the earth

It's lucky we can glance
at the sky

or we would all have
shrunk to ant size

Dimensional heart
dimensional thinking

Magnificent seeing
as focused as a pinpoint

or a surgeon teasing out a
lymphatic polyp from next to

an internal jugular
without nicking the vein

Our shadows don't tell us who we are
our sheer spiritual genius does

"Go fetch water from the river" one
teacher said

and the student lived an entire lifetime
until one day he noticed

he'd not moved from the riverbank
and his water jug was overflowing

On the one hand all's a dream
on the other the dream leads to wisdom

and back far enough from what we
press our noses to

we see the beached whale by an
ocean in its earthly basin

for almost an eternity

sloshing among the
placid stars

12/18
(Jeffrson Hospital
night after right neck dissection)

SKY DIVER

What does the sky diver see at first?
His own nothingness or the

nothingness of space?

Is he hurtling or is the
earth hurtling toward him?

Does the face behind the sky
pull aside its mask?

Has light become his element
so he's light

passing through light?

Speed is nothing

I imagine it's like not
moving at all

Yet velocity reigns supreme

The more we go
do we become less of ourselves

or more?

What a shame at the
end of the day to be

stuck with just yourself
when radiance is so

close at hand

The lion's last crunch
should be a blissful burst

Everything that's past
long gone and

ever present

sweetly lost and wandering
in the Ever-Presence of

God

We've only got so much time
to make that leap

But it's not a matter of time

Free falling through the air at
those altitudes

timeless

and at that point
what does it matter

who's falling towards whom?

12/18
(Jefferson Hospital,
night after surgery)

HOSPITAL WINDOW

The night outside this hospital window
sits very still

What does it know of what takes place
behind these walls?

The agony and the ecstasy

The long lit corridors with
nurses dutifully shuffling quickly

and the expert doctors and the frauds

We're all frauds

What do we know about the
movements of the soul inside the body?

That it looks out and sees
white tents pitched for

miles on a pebbly plain?

How do we listen to the
mechanism that tells us

exactly where to press where to
cut where to splice

inside the total enigma of
mortal being?

Nothing races away from us
It's all here

Signals look at us with
compassionate eyes

Broken down or breaking down
we're still whole

Somehow we're always
children with faces

pressed against a window

our hearts
thumping with excitement

12/19
(3 a.m. Jefferson Hospital)

BIG BOAT

I think existence's big boat sits on a mirror
lake of uttermost elegance

at the top of the world
with a silver circle of terns scintillating

always in motion above it
like an incandescent halo that is actually

the bottom of a perpetual angelic machinery
seen from below

that casts on the deck aurora borealis
cloth-shivering patterns whispering

away into nothingness and coming back
full force to enwrap us

enthralled in its folds minute after
minute each moment giving us the

illusion of time's movement in
any direction outward

from God's elegant center

12/23

ROBINSON CRUSOE DIPS HIS FOOT

1

Robinson Crusoe dips his foot in the river
checking for piranhas

watches the grasses of the glade
checking for vipers

squats in the tallest tree branches
checking for cougars

barely relaxes at twilight or dawn
cocking his ears at every crack or twitch

in the air around him
squinching his eyes nearly shut

snapping them open at the next sound

his whole being shocked alert at his
very existence in this new world

in this next life after drowning

Shipwreck his mind on the shoals leaving
just enough provisions

having to ferry them to shore and then

inland to his invented habitation

visited by toucans and gibbons
and a crawling earth all around him

ready to pounce

He's Adam naming his solitude
and he names it *Despair* then amends it in

time as time goes on
to *Endurance* then gradually to

Survival then to *Watchful Subsistence*
then *The Emperor of Nothingness*

King of All He Surveys
loss upon loss

until nothing is left
(and it's not even Friday)

and blue sky hangs above him
like a bell ringing for

him alone
bereft now only of

bereftness itself

soul hitting its highest pitch

and dazzling there

2

Crusoe found himself
where he'd never been before

just as we do
going where we go

Surrounded by exotic foliage and
hot turquoise waves lapping

blackened shores under beaten sun and
leavened moonlight

alternating

So it's no wonder he at first couldn't
recognize himself when he met himself in

Friday's form not the living
shadow of himself but his

real self of which Crusoe himself
was just the

bleached holy ghost of the
unity of the two of them

lost together on a
single island

two atrial valves on either side
propelling

in the sea's tumultuous breast

3

"The revelation of the Face of God
is from within the

events of our lives"
thought Crusoe alone in his

aloneness

neither slave nor king of all he
surveys

but a soul within that "within-ness"
and a soul apart

seeing with the single
eye of his heart

4

The island Crusoe lived on
became the hat he wore

and the shoes he wrapped around his
feet

the arterial streams his arteries
and the ocean the world at large

He'd been on all the peaks and
looked down every sheer cliff

Birds scattered at his noise
and when he held his breath

the air snapped shut
and life took center stage

He was the drama of a
lost soul under the stars

His thoughts were the
unobtainable gazelle that

leapt over the ridge
into the long lush valley below

It's true he gave up thinking of escape
or dreaming of flight

but as he entered anonymity among the
dull rocks and stones

the winds and stalks
his light one of the fragile candles

another kind of darkness became
his darkness

Loving fingers of it from behind around his
middle that

stretched him out at night
a night he seemed to be

transported through the air in
from ocean to ocean

side to side of his
own islanded sides

and the sides of the world
the full dimension

sprung from form
whose island as he rose

disappeared from
under him

12/24

BIG SOAP LITTLE SOAP

The big soap washes the big body
The little soap washes the little body

From the veils of heaven the big soap
foams for use

The little soap you rub and rub and a few
bubbles come out

For the big soap you need tympani and a few
trumpet riffs

The little soap does quite nicely with a
short piano run and maybe a

harmonica note or two

All kinds of celestial colors cross and
mix in the big soap's foam

When that foam touches your body
you take on rainbow hues

Lather it up and you're a canyon of
gorgeous sunrises and sunsets

Even savage beasts look like
angels

All the mesquite bushes look like the
Lote Tree of the Farthest Limit of Matter in

This World beyond which
only the most exalted pass

and the Prophet alone *(peace be upon him)*
continues on and on

alone at the Throne

Rub a dub dub with the little soap
when you need a wash

thoroughly serviceable for a quick
turnaround

The deep heart in all this
can't get enough of it big or little

You start with a dry bar
and end with an ocean of Light

12/28

PINHOLE

Is our life any more than a pinhole
in the great cloth of the stars?

All its angular dramatics any more than
the licking of paws of a cat before it

curls up to sleep?

And as we head towards that pinhole
inexorably forward with the

brightest of faces and the bravest and
stoutest of hearts

an entire lifetime's worth
able to go through that

hole to the other side

every thought thought word
spoken or left unspoken

meandering or unmeandering
heartache

and as we slip through and see the
other side for what it is

do we know the brilliant
significance of our

being before God's gazillion-dimensional
space in every

direction possible conceptually impossible
in which we also fly to

all the reaches
stretched beyond mortality

to a brilliantly burning single
living flame?

I mean seriously
we face the pinhole

on this side of it
our shadows cast against the

surface of its surroundings
knowing one day we'll

have to go through it

with our hearts realizing
we should try to be on

both sides of it at once
right now

that special anointed
halo-headed projection

forward

in the great
cloth of the stars

12/29

FROM A PARTICULAR HEIGHT

From a particular height
a stone bird is sought

From another altitude
silk rain's beseeched

From yet another more daring
God's outline in the dark

His perspective from a peak
over all the world

The heart like a pinnacle
scaled in a blink

blind the outer eye
the inner eye opened

The journey entailing
a wholehearted silence

the iciness warmed
by the charge of our blood

We come back with nothing
and no words to say it

more precious than all the

things we can name

all radiance captured
in uncapturable space

the subtlest lineaments
of His indescribable Face

A door opened quietly
the whole room dissolved

The house dark at last
and everyone sleeping

The whisper that lights up
the five known worlds

This and the next
and the three realms between

Mulk Malakut Jabarut
at the tips of our heartbeats

vision soft as a feather
enfolding the moon

We sit very still
and it all comes inside us

The altitudes turned
into generous gestures

Open hand for the horses
to nibble sugar in bliss

in the barn where the owl sits
as darkness comes down

Take from the silence
what words you can

Add your silence and they rise
to their proper dimensions

From a particular height
where a stone bird is sought

from another altitude
where silk rain's beseeched

and from another more daring
God's outline in the dark

His perspective from a peak
over all the worlds

12/30

BARKING DOG

I fall asleep to a barking dog
and wake up to the same dog

still barking

Have the Towers fallen again
in the thousand years between?

Angela Lansbury still introduces
everything British

Rivers flow with garbage
then flow clear

I think Hawaii still floats out west
under a green sky

Uncle Dorwinkle falls asleep in his chair
and the chair holds still

Sadness hangs over us like rain
and wets us with its mercy

There's no accounting for taste
in the smörgasbord of emotions

The cosmos rolls up a hill that
doesn't exist then

rolls down it again

Every gnat lives its allotted lifespan
in a *whizz bang* of energy

We go forward with our hands at our
sides or out in front

depending on our sense of security
in God's wondrous arranging

Ah!

The dog has stropped barking
but it's not the end of me

1/13

ONE DAY

One day day crowed itself awake
and woke the rooster up

The sun shone without explosions from
inside and maintained its galactic hold

The moon became luminous on its own for a
moment without reflecting the sun

Are any of these things possible?
That we become available to blessings

from He Who distributes blessings
with no effort on our part

but only by being cradled in the
luminosity of creation

suspended in the hammock of our being
between the two dark trees at either end of us

bathed in its bath continually
from the heart outward?

This rubbery flesh around our bones
enough of light?

What we so long for and head toward

with us all the time?

Are we the fish in the sea
who wishes it were

surrounded by water?

Do birds look at us and
envy how hard we trod the ground?

On the peaks of the earth
emerged from the waters

do we long for dry land?

Since birth luminosity is unavoidable
unless we shut it all down

The back of the throat of
that which swallows us

shimmers with light!

1/2

THE FACT IS

The fact is
the brilliant irreducible fact is

donkeys stand still against a green
hillside enamored of the

day's beauty and the oncoming
velvety protection of night

Swallows dip their wings as they swoop
from eaves to treetops and we

wonder if it's their language or
their sheer genius of

aeronautics

A trail goes up a hill that's been zigzaggedly
laid down by so many before us who are

no longer walking it yet each of their
footfalls helped pound its unruly atoms smooth

and the fact that everything is just as it
is though perhaps not enough as

explanation yet serves as a key to all
meaning and the virtual

iridescence of things

intimating that behind or within them and
behind our ocular or even conceptualized

seeing lies a realer reality infused with the
incessant cascade of its own light

and not just one universe more than we
see but a revolving diamond of

universes whose one facet's surface we
perceive each moment turning

as a fleck of light raises its camera

slowly or rapidly behind
the palpable showing us

first one facet then another
then another and another

each one stamped with the Creator's
indelible signature decipherable only by the

light of the Prophet *(peace be upon him)*
whose consciousness accompanies

and is at the root essence of
every living thing without end

amen

1/3

OH LORD

Oh Lord
if we die roll us in a crystal barrel

over a waterfall of light

Shade us under a tree of sparklers
each one bigger than the stars

and twice as bright

Stand us in a galloping of horses
faster than stillness and far more

silent than night

The swallower has a hold on us
and would swallow us

if not for your magnetic
mercifulness that covers our

erratic imperfections and sets them
right

If we live let us never again look at
anything but Your Face

with trillion-dimensional insight

1/5

WHY AM I STILL ALIVE?

for Ruhiye Dell

Why am I still alive?

Does a gold wheel roll down
a gold hill?

The screech of a parrot in her cage
wakes the neighbors up

Wild horses chomp grass in a
nearby dale

The sky is always purple
around this time of day

Whispers pass from mouth to ear
and back again

When you use up all your minutes
you've still got seconds to go

Flamingos in flocks across the sun
make an unusual silhouette

I could have died back there
under the knife

One nick on the jugular
and blood would have flowed

There's an echo that goes back in time
to the first shout made

A whale's eye on one side of its head
on the other side its other eye

gives it a whale's eye view for sure

I wouldn't trade my life for its own
with anything else in earth or heaven

Close the gate when you go

Come back another time
when time's gone fishing

in God's lake

1/6

THE CHIRR OF THE MOTORS

The *chirr* of the motors and the
rattletrap constellation

The *chugga chug* of the
pistons driving it all and the

angelic singing in the stems of leaves
the light xylophone bonging of

waters hitting rocks or
tumbling out of faucets

The high hum of space itself happily
embracing its spaciousness

Things folding over and over each
other and folding underneath and

across

If looked at from one angle as
thin as a hair

If looked at from another the whole
bulge of our solar galaxy gurgling in the

Milky Way

Click clack of all matter as it
clatters from its formation to its demise

Atoms themselves intoning the most
sacred sounds in the ascending

temples of their exact positions in time
on the edges and at the cores of

everything

Then crescendos and diminuendos
sometimes simultaneous with the

elegant but static melody going on
incessantly inside it

and now on our lips in praise of it
to the God Who put its raw

articulation always beyond our
reach but that we

never tire trying to catch
in the silence of awe

that surrounds us

1/7

HOW DO WE EFFLORESCE

How do we effloresce the ineffable

and I don't mean anything too
arcane or even mystical

The snarl of a tiger
The sleek sheen of a gazelle's back

sliding through sunlight

What processes go on unnoticed
inside us all the time awake or

asleep

Blood circulation that keeps going
round and round

ascending and descending through us

The inelegant as well as
elegant breaths we take and

exhale in gorgeousness or monstrousness
as backdrops of jungles and

alleyways drop away

leaving us standing under the stars
ineffably and efflorescently alive

falling outward into nothingness
and the air all around us

1/11

I UNDRESS FOR BED

I undress for bed and
take off my arms and legs my

breast and breath
and all internal organs until there's a

door in the air I go through in
heart's light to where

no bodies dwell well or not
winning or losing

trudge and welter
sweltering or chilled

but an argosy of air a
straight fairway of atmosphere where each

nothingness is tinged with
rainbows of gold

there where our true hearts lie
in their dizzying rotations within

light upon light

1/14

RED WAGONS

If through this one
all the world's billion or so

red wagons were presented to
ransom this poem or even

one hair of this poem not even yet
written nor even conceptualized in

heart/mind complex
now presently in motion

and this lined page of my notebook
on which I write these poems though

still half-blank although its

blank half is slowly being shortened as I
write lines of this poem line by line

I say if all the world's red
wagons were lined up in exchange for it

it not budge from its invisible
sovereignty nor even enter

negotiations sight unseen on behalf of
this unwritten as yet poem in

progress no matter where those
wagons may be from say glorious

Italian ones with hand painted roses
or Mongolian sled wagons maybe

pulled by dogs or deer

some modern flashy wagons assembled in
Tokyo or even prehistoric ones

from an archeological dig in Jordan
filled with important pictographs —

that none be taken for this though
as yet unwritten poem even as it's

being written

no matter how gleaming or
freshly painted how swift or sleek

There! I think we're
done here —

Don't even let me hear the
squeak of their tires on

cobblestone roads or the soft
metal clatter of metal-wheeled wagons

taken back off down
dark streets home —

Keep your
red wagons

This poem
is done

1/15

I'M NOT SURE IF DEATH

I'm not sure if death is a cliff
or an invisible chair made of

real rock

A leap on the back of a sleek beast
over ripples that might be

flames or clouds

or a man in livery taking us on our first
chauffeured ride in a long low car

to a border guard where it's we
who are stamped

not passports

I'm not sure if death comes in for us
or we go out for it

generously and agreed —

After living a whole life however
short

is death a musical note sung by a
zillion voice choir ranged on a

landscape not unlike the
Grand Canyon

but in sharper colors?

Or a long low whistling corridor of ice
we run a long long time in

to a vividly imagined destination
with lots of huge slow buffalo grazing

Technicolor grass

and a wise elephant
standing stock still?

Is it a series of doorways
only one of which we fit through

or do we even get up for it?

It's instantaneous acceptance at the
border and we're suddenly there

to an aroma of sizzling olive oil and freshly
brewed coffee?

Or we're not sure we've even budged from our
spot but

everything's different and in a

different key

people talking in a
different voice register saying

completely different things we've
never heard before

but that we understand completely

Death is something that perhaps for the
first time in all our lives for sure we know is

really happening to us alone with pure
intensity

not quite airborne

not quite earthbound

a sled slid across the sky

a long low sigh

1/17

DEATH CANOE

Curled inside the canoe of death
I hear my life played forward

through mists hanging above a
very black lake

Call and reply from shore to shore
crossing above me in the gray

watery screen
and their echoes

crossing above me
where nothing else stirs

I can picture it all
as it moves along

in excruciating detail
steep hill of solid rock

amid the crumbling realities

floating their images like
honey bees

as it moves forward

all around me

1/21

AT THE GATE

What is the payment expected at the Gate?
Blood droplets leading here — *exertions*

We see through the grille work that is
ourselves what's on the

other side
more splendid than we thought

breathtaking speechlessness
leaping in steady slow motion through

everything

The transparent everything that was
always around us

What are those profiles in shadow
those voices in light?

And I sit in a small warm
room in winter and

write this

eyes closed
heart pulsing

Row house neighbors' voices
heard through the wall 3:30 a.m.

Eighteen degrees outside

Aware that everything next
is already here

not fluffily but specifically
charted

at this flashpoint of being
sending forward what we

already have
in us

all the green poplars blue streams
and incandescent flamingoes

unrolling in the nowhere
we currently inhabit

where death simply
notes our arrival

on schedule
antler mask discarded

at the gate
glad pipes playing

blood droplets dissolved
in our exertions

1/24

FASTER THAN LIGHT

The hinges and latches that
connect the soul to the body

The strings snaps hooks pins flanges
rotating cogs tiny perfect

buttons sutures laces staples
that connect the soul to the body

even under water
even in free fall midair

The bolts pegs nails screws
locks braids ropes cinches

sheaths of microscopic stitches
cross-stitched anatomical embroidery

The seamless continuous texture
that doesn't show where

one starts and the other leaves off
even in a dark wood with hoot owls

at the moment of death
at the moment of birth

Who is this person we are?

Why are we not blown apart
at the slightest wind?

Why must love permeate the two of us
to one evanescent unity?

We dance — the two of us —
around a single pivot

God's love holding us

We vanish —
God's love still
holding us

The soul leaves at last

This world's body like this world
becomes bone meal

and all the fasteners unfasten
and so too our fascination

as we sing the soul song
all the way home

to the soul's home
faster than light

1/26

I'M GOING UP A VERY ROCKY STEPLADDER

I'm going up a very rocky
stepladder to God

First I lost the fish that would have
won me first prize and now I'm

down here with Gilgamesh diving for the
divine lotus with pink-gummed grinning

sharks all around us

And then the crack of dawn that's more than
once found me asleep under a Monet

haystack with more gold than even
Rumpelstiltskin can harp into being

My legs won't work and my heart is
more than a lonely hunter among the

prehistoric bric-a-brac of the
twenty-first century

Why I've lost bone marrow I never owned
and respect I've never warranted

But little goldfish jump in my pockets
and there's a canary in my right sleeve

waiting for just the right time to
come out and sing the

one note that
explains it all

I'm going up a very rocky
stepladder past the

Sistine Chapel cartoons by
Al Capp better known for

L'il Abner

Yet here it all is in symphonic panoply
the entire mortal ceiling under which we so

piously dwell and above which all the
planetary galaxies in their whistling

space overcoats and
flexing their gravitational pulleys

whirr and whirl in their
elliptical orbits

and the shadows they cast as they pass
are what we take for real life on

this as on every other planet in the

universa-sphere where

exact same human forms are going about their
business carving lives out for themselves on the

only flowering crystal tree's already overcrowded
bark but where there's always miraculously

room made for a zillion more

One step at a time
ignoring this world

up and up past it all

with a sweet wave and a thrown kiss

I'm going up a very rocky
stepladder to God

1/29

OF THE PEWTER GLEAM

Of the pewter gleam crossing the opposite wall
and the ripple of horses leaping the low hedge

and the sound of running water everywhere
even when you close your ears

and the expanding silence everywhere
no sound interrupts

and the majestic height from the ground to the
top of his head when he appears

and the length of the shadow he casts across
the uneven ground when he appears

and the withdrawal of all imagery
back through the siphon of its origin

and the lacquered checkerboard table
on the top floor of the castle a ray of

sunlight hits through a tall arched window
during the poorly attended beheading taking

place in the courtyard below
while ocean waves roar their mighty roars

only a mile or two from here at the shore

and herons fly across the sun at twilight

and centuries later none of us remembers
except that for certain details

everything's remained the same
the sound of water everywhere the same

horses leaping the hedges the same
sunlight hitting a surface through a

tall window the same
the irony of a death hardly

anyone notices
clutching at a last appeal for God's clemency

and receiving it or not

the same

2/1

A NOTE SO TENUOUS

A note so tenuous you can
barely hear it in the dark

and then there's space itself in seeming
silence with its subtle fabric of tones

and doorways that
let out into starry space

and others that let in ravenous tigers
before you have a chance to react

and down on the street the
hurdy gurdy man with monkey or a

security system car horn with its
ear-splitting one note sustained

Then the whispered command of a
superior officer to detonate the bomb

and the hush afterwards
that reaches to the bottom of the sea

and the throne of God where
sound originates and

dissipates at the same time

a window closing out the world
and a window letting in the

world's light and air
and the room transformed

the person inside
revived by it and sitting up

the walls seeming to breathe with
new life and the windows expanding

and outside an eagle catching a mouse with
one swoop

and grass bending in autumn wind
and things falling from trees

cones leaves branches boughs nests
people onto the

hard ground forever
and the hush afterwards

and the long hush after that

2/3

AFTER WISDOM

After wisdom there's
blue stars in an ochre sky

After wisdom there are mountains who
get up on their hind legs and

howl at the moon

After wisdom there's a
young boy herding an unruly ox

who bends to his will

After wisdom there's the
usual rainbows when tea is

poured from an iron pot into a
porcelain cup

After wisdom wide eyes of
animals appear to blush

A light surrounds everything
blending into nothing at all

After wisdom gates open
squeakily as well as noiselessly

After wisdom a kind of polished stainless steel
doorframe surrounds every passageway

Cities come and go but grasses and
rivers remain

Night follows day in the usual way
as dogs follow their masters

happy to serve

After wisdom
no words describe it nor is there any

inclination to do so

Bridges start at the far end of space
and end at the other

The steps we take are always
modest and meaningful

The breaths we breathe are the
same place rainbows come from

After wisdom comes
sitting in a chair

and being there

2/4

A PARTICULAR ROTATION

A particular rotation brings us back to
ourselves up inside ourselves like

owlets looking out the bark hole from their
nests inside onto the light of day

among the first days of their lives

If we breathe in all the way from the
sea's horizon and its rolls of surf

inwardly rolling toward us
we may also have such

first days again and look with
first eyes onto first things afresh

Even Galapagos lizards blink in the sun
as they barely move in the heat

alone on the spikes of earthly extremity
poking out of the sea

The whole universe gets drawn up inside
us one breath at a time

with its rotating glitter of lights whose
rapid flashes blink the Divine Names

in perfect succession to spell out the
alphabet of everything that is and

will be holding itself erotically closer
to what appears this very moment

all over the world first day after
first day under its canopy of

starlings and swooping gulls

its stars and curving curls of
momentarily

stationary cloud

2/9

HAVING LEANT DOWN

Having leant down to deliver
then leant back up again

leaving the deliverer bewildered
and the world of heavy objects

just as plentiful

Oasis trees blowing their heavy fronds
and dunes moving particle by particle

elsewhere

and the sky now so blue it hurts

and the deliverer among us
dispensing fresh light from his

food basket

and fresh food from his
suspended basket of fresh light

2/9

PRAISE OF ALLAH

Praise of Allah is the
ticket that purchases entrance

How can we know His true worth
who can't assess the immediate with

surety though we
cast our eyes in

search of Him outside the
place of His true habitation?

Where He doesn't reside
but where we've been told His

power is
and we see from here His

incandescence falling against the
things we know and

throwing the things of this world we know
into shadow

The eye's retina itself a goldfish bowl
whose visions call us to our knees

in awe

2/12

INDEX

ABOUT THE AUTHOR

Born in 1940 in Oakland, California, Daniel Abdal-Hayy Moore had his first book of poems, *Dawn Visions*, published by Lawrence Ferlinghetti of City Lights Books, San Francisco, in 1964, and the second in 1972, *Burnt Heart/Ode to the War Dead.* He created and directed *The Floating Lotus Magic Opera Company* in Berkeley, California in the late 60s, and presented two major productions, *The Walls Are Running Blood,* and *Bliss Apocalypse.* He became a Sufi Muslim in 1970, performed the Hajj in 1972, and lived and traveled throughout Morocco, Spain, Algeria and Nigeria, landing in California and publishing *The Desert is the Only Way Out,* and *Chronicles of Akhira* in the early 80s (Zilzal Press). Residing in Philadelphia since 1990, in 1996 he published *The Ramadan Sonnets* (Jusoor/City Lights), and in 2002, *The Blind Beekeeper* (Jusoor/ Syracuse University Press). He has been the major editor for a number of works, including *The Burdah* of Shaykh Busiri, translated by Hamza Yusuf, and the poetry of Palestinian poet, Mahmoud Darwish, translated by Munir Akash. He is also widely published on the worldwide web: *The American Muslim, DeenPort,* and his own website and poetry blog, among others: *www.danielmoorepoetry.com, www.ecstaticxchange.wordpress.com.* He has been poetry editor for *Seasons Journal, Islamica Magazine,* a 2010 translation by Munir Akash of *State of Siege*, by Mahmoud Darwish (Syracuse University Press), and *The Prayer of the Oppressed,* by Imam Muhammad Nasir al-Dar'i, translated by Hamza Yusuf. In 2011 and 2012 he was a winner of the Nazim Hikmet Prize for Poetry. *The Ecstatic Exchange Series* is bringing out the extensive body of his works of poetry (a complete list of published works on page 2).

POETIC WORKS by Daniel Abdal-Hayy Moore
Published and Unpublished

Dawn Visions (published by City Lights, 1964)
Burnt Heart/Ode to the War Dead (published by City Lights, 1972)
This Body of Black Light Gone Through the Diamond (printed by Fred Stone, Cambridge, Mass, 1965)
On The Streets at Night Alone (1965?)
All Hail the Surgical Lamp (1967)
States of Amazement (1970)

Abdallah Jones and the Disappearing-Dust Caper (published by The Ecstatic Exchange/Crescent Series, 2006)
'Ala ud-Deen and the Magic Lamp (published by The Ecstatic Exchange, 2011)
The Chronicles of Akhira (1981) (published by Zilzal Press with Typoglyphs by Karl Kempton, 1986; published in Sparrow on the Prophet's Tomb by The Ecstatic Exchange, 2009)
Mouloud (1984) (A Zilzal Press chapbook, 1995; published in Sparrow on the Prophet's Tomb by The Ecstatic Exchange, 2009)
Man is the Crown of Creation (1984)
The Look of the Lion (The Parabolas of Sight) (1984)
The Desert is the Only Way Out (completed 4/21/84) (Zilzal Press chapbook, 1985)
Atomic Dance (1984) (am here books, 1988)
Outlandish Tales (1984)
Awake as Never Before (12/26/84) (Zilzal Press chapbook, 1993)
Glorious Intervals (1/1/85) (Zilzal Press chapbook, ?)
Long Days on Earth/Book I (1/28 – 8/30/85)
Long Days on Earth/Book II (Hayy Ibn Yaqzan)
Long Days on Earth/Book III (1/22/86)
Long Days on Earth/Book IV (1986)
The Ramadan Sonnets (Long Days on Earth/Book V) (5/9 – 6/11/86) (published by Jusoor/City Lights Books, 1996) (republished as Ramadan Sonnets by The Ecstatic Exchange, 2005)
Long Days on Earth/Book VI (6-8/30/86)
Holograms (9/4/86 – 3/26/87)
History of the World (The Epic of Man's Survival) (4/7 – 6/18/87)
Exploratory Odes (6/25 – 10/18/87)

The Man at the End of the World (11/11 – 12/10/87)
The Perfect Orchestra (3/30 – 7/25/88)(published by The Ecstatic Exchange, 2009)
Fed from Underground Springs (7/30 – 11/23/88)
Ideas of the Heart (11/27/88 – 5/5/89)
New Poems (scattered poems, out of series, from 3/24 – 8/9/89)
Facing Mecca (5/16 – 11/11/89)
A Maddening Disregard for the Passage of Time (11/17/89 – 5/20/90) (published by The Ecstatic Exchange, 2009)
The Heart Falls in Love with Visions of Perfection (6/15/90 – 6/2/91)
Like When You Wave at a Train and the Train Hoots Back at You (Farid's Book) (6/11 – 7/26/91) (published by The Ecstatic Exchange, 2008)
Orpheus Meets Morpheus (8/1/91– 3/14/92)
The Puzzle (3/21/92 – 8/17/93)(published by The Ecstatic Exchange, 2011)
The Greater Vehicle (10/17/93 – 4/30/94)
A Hundred Little 3-D Pictures (5/14/94 – 9/11/95)
The Angel Broadcast (9/29 – 12/17/95)
Mecca/Medina Time-Warp (12/19/95 – 1/6/96) (published as a Zilzal Press chapbook, 1996)(published in Sparrow on the Prophet's Tomb, 2009)
Miracle Songs for the Millennium (1/20 – 10/16/96)
The Blind Beekeeper (11/15/96 – 5/30/97) (published 2002 by Jusoor/Syracuse University Press)
Chants for the Beauty Feast (6/3 – 10/28/97)(published by The Ecstatic Exchange, 2011
You Open a Door and it's a Starry Night (10/29/97 – 5/23/98) (published by The Ecstatic Exchange, 2009)
Salt Prayers (5/29 – 10/24/98) (published by The Ecstatic Exchange, 2005)
Some (10/25/98 – 4/25/99)
Flight to Egypt (5/1 – 5/16/99)
I Imagine a Lion (5/21 – 11/15/99) (published by The Ecstatic Exchange, 2006)
Millennial Prognostications (11/25/99 – 2/2/2000) (published by the Ecstatic Exchange, 2009)
Shaking the Quicksilver Pool (2/4 – 10/8/2000) (published by The Ecstatic Exchange, 2009)
Blood Songs (10/9/2000 – 4/3/2001)(Published by The Ecstatic Exchange, 2012)
The Music Space (4/10 – 9/16/2001) (published by The Ecstatic Exchange, 2007)
Where Death Goes (9/20/2001 – 5/1/2002) (published by The Ecstatic Exchange, 2009)

The Flame of Transformation Turns to Light (99 Ghazals Written in English) (5/14 – 8/21/2002) (published by The Ecstatic Exchange, 2007)
Through Rose-Colored Glasses (7/22/2002 – 1/15/2003) (published by The Ecstatic Exchange, 2007)
Psalms for the Broken-Hearted (1/22 – 5/25/2003) (published by The Ecstatic Exchange, 2006)
Hoopoe's Argument (5/27 – 9/18/03)
Love is a Letter Burning in a High Wind (9/21 – 11/6/2003) (published by The Ecstatic Exchange, 2006)
Laughing Buddha/Weeping Sufi (11/7/2003 – 1/10/2004) (published by The Ecstatic Exchange, 2005)
Mars and Beyond (1/20 – 3/29/2004) (published by The Ecstatic Exchange, 2005)
Underwater Galaxies (4/5 – 7/21/2004) (published by The Ecstatic Exchange, 2007)
Cooked Oranges (7/23/2004 – 1/24/2005 (published by The Ecstatic Exchange, 2007)
Holiday from the Perfect Crime (1/25 – 6/11/2005)(published by The Ecstatic Exchange, 2011)
Stories Too Fiery to Sing Too Watery to Whisper (6/13 – 10/24/2005)
Coattails of the Saint (10/26/2005 – 5/10/2006) (published by The Ecstatic Exchange, 2006)
In the Realm of Neither (5/14/2006 – 11/12/06) (published by The Ecstatic Exchange, 2008)
Invention of the Wheel (11/13/06 – 6/10/07)(published by The Ecstatic Exchange, 2010)
The Sound of Geese Over the House (6/15 – 11/4/07)
The Fire Eater's Lunchbreak (11/11/07 – 5/19/2008) (published by The Ecstatic Exchange, 2008)
Sparks Off the Main Strike (5/24/2008 – 1/10/2009)(published by The Ecstatic Exchange, 2010)
Stretched Out on Amethysts (1/13 – 9/17/2009)(published by The Ecstatic Exchange, 2010)
The Throne Perpendicular to All that is Horizontal (9/18/09 – 1/25/10)
In Constant Incandescence (2/10 – 8/13/10) (published by The Ecstatic Exchange, 2011)
The Caged Bear Spies the Angel (8/30/10 – 3/6/11)(published by The Ecstatic Exchange, 2010)

This Light Slants Upward (3/7 – 10/13/11)
Ramadan is Burnished Sunlight (part of This Light Slants Upward, published separately by The Ecstatic Exchange, 2011)
The Match That Becomes a Conflagration (10/14/11 – 5/9/12)
Down at the Deep End (5/10 – 8/3/12) (published by The Ecstatic Exchange, 2012)
Next Life (8/9/12 – 2/12/13) (published by The Ecstatic Exchange, 2013)

www.ingramcontent.com/pod-product-compliance
Lightning Source LLC
Chambersburg PA
CBHW032043150426
43194CB00006B/405
9780578120225